ALANIS MORISSETTE

Jake Wild Hall is an award-winning poet and one half of Bad Betty Press. He has performed on BBC Radio and at festivals and literary events across the UK. He is a multiple slam champion, and his work has been published in magazines, anthologies, and online journals. He is the author of two pamphlets: *Solomon's World*, which was longlisted for the Saboteur Award for Best Pamphlet, and *Blank*.

He has worked with partners including Penguin, Apples and Snakes, Writing East Midlands, Derby Poetry Festival, and Pearson. He has also been a guest tutor at Nottingham Trent University, the University of Nottingham, King's College London, the University of Lincoln, and others.

This is his debut collection.

Also by Jake Wild Hall

CONTENTS

All the houses in you

The first sound after silence

It's not death anymore just Gary Lineker

For Granny Kate, Gboyega, Caz, and Dean
and all the poets who made me, who won't get to read this book.

ISBN: 978-1-917617-57-4

Cover designed by Aaron Kent

Edited and Typeset by Aaron Kent

Broken Sleep Books Ltd
PO BOX 102
Llandysul
SA44 9BG

Alanis Morissette

Jake Wild Hall

Broken Sleep Books

not understanding a prayer is no reason not to say amen
— Gboyega Odubanjo

All the houses in you

The day begins

with a small

flutter through

a closed fist

then stops

WORMWOOD

the classic Cadbury's chocolate bar the Chomp

reminds me of visiting my dad in prison

scrunch of wrapper   slow mechanic door clank

we were sent Christmas to unwrap on vhs

replaying it so often the tape crackles and wears

until it becomes a foreboding

a fizzy thinning thing a cut to black

eventually all dads die this way

      visiting my dad in prison

    Christmas   on vhs

   so often the tape   wears

  becomes a foreboding

a fizzy thinning   cut to black

eventually all dads die this way

    visiting

    Christmas   on vhs

     the tape   wears

  becomes   foreboding

                        cut to black

eventually all dads die this way

            Christmas

                        tape   wears

        becomes

                        a cut to black

eventually all dads die

REFUGE

I am so many days light in the liver

smudge biscuit crumb into my jeans

I have been hopeless with strangers

in a room above a church

the world is ending and I must know

in every hour of the day I have memory

my daughter says I love you more

still seeks maternal at bedtime

maybe all the times I chose one thing

over everything are a fish bone in her throat

as a kid I played one touch against myself

made a thousand imaginary friends

the day after *All Good?* skipped on the record player

we watched new plates be put on the shelf

my sister left a note in my palm before

she climbed out of her own childhood

am I protecting my children

and myself from the same thing?

I go upstairs and make sure they are still

breathing turn off my son's audiobook

check if my daughter needs the toilet

ask her to koala on me when she says yes

TWO DEAD MEN WALK INTO A ROOM

the one I remember

holds me close to sky

juggles fire over me

and my sister   contraband

stuffed petrol tank

a woman breaking

the one everyone remembers

naked and blue smiling

on a front page making

Christmas happen after

a sentence   a paycheque

a small relief strapped

to a quickening heartbeat

I don't know how I'd have lived

with you if your funeral

didn't offer a redemption arc

you found me difficult to love

maybe too much mirror

when I remember you

I find it difficult to love

maybe too many lessons

I could have been a rib

I could have been a throat

you could have been the car

you could have been the cell

I could have been you

ALANIS MORISSETTE

small dark speck on the window

looks at me says you are lonely

small dark speck on the window

laughs   you are surrounded by joy

small dark speck on the window

stares at me how it stares

small dark speck on the window won't go away

I scrub till my hands bleed

small dark speck becomes smudge

small dark smudge on the window

small dark smudge becomes smear

small dark smear on the window

small dark smear becomes window

small dark window

small dark window becomes house

small dark house becomes me

small dark me in the corner

tea goes cold on the window sill

I ask Alanis Morissette the meaning of irony

haha she says and disappears

I turn my phone on and hate myself

I turn it off that's a lie

I have fallen down like Alice

I am *drink me* size in my stomach

VII

chips radiate in the microwave

        Ifrit is called forth

                rises from Cloud's command

        every win a fleeting dream

   somewhere your dad is being released

you wait for a comet on a white background

it is holier and won't be long

until he leaves again

             for what we don't know is the last time

there will be no avalanche of emotion when

a white orb falls from your dad

  rejoins the lifestream

you will only wonder why Aerith's theme doesn't play

as the conveyor belt nudges him offscreen

wonder if Nabou Uematsu would have made this moment

more memorable maybe   there

would have been more strings and less folk music

would the frame rate be different

    is this just the scratch on the second disc that forces you to

reset

A POEM ABOUT ONIONS

I have been watching 2am break in to a screech a harsh reality
an echo have slowly been peeling layers off me and saying it's
fine because it is and who needs so many layers anyway I've
always had enough of myself to give more away surely this is
why I created a person

ALED JONES

Path dissipating with our footsteps
satsumas melting in our mouths
child's gloves slick with ice
the skyline is merry
breath settling on nothing
we gather the cold
into the shape of a man
i hand my child a nose
raise her to shoulder height

taxi fizzles in our eyeline

NO MAN IS

cutting yourself into yourself

trying to make memory a reality

some people say you were a party

the wrong side of midnight

when you are in this house it is as a ghost

when you were in this house it was a haunting

one night me and my sister are told

we can stay up till the night tucks us in

in return we carry bags

the hope   that no blue lights reach

into our pockets and take tomorrow from us

I wonder if all the houses in you weighed you down

it's not long until you will have been

gone longer than you were here

seven years ago I aged past you

what is the word for a living ghost?

RECESS

end of the holidays I would   to my parents they would   with
sandwiches   sweep my long unpopular   my eyes and remind me
it is easy to forget   every day someone you would like to be friends
they don't want to   says   isn't it funny that your dad   I am   to
this day hiding all my   in the way I   and pick and   myself   to
cover   with plasters and stories   just anxiety just born that way
as a kid wouldn't muddy my wellies   it is easy to forget   when
you have found   people who were waiting   probably don't
think   don't ask   certain things until one day daughter says they
didn't   and boy said and   I say   wife I will   his dad and call
mum and   says   probably won't help   imagine you can't see
but   deep breath   try to   and   please it's okay   and I love
you and   sip water   are you ok?

DYING FOR BEGINNERS
After Kathryn Mannix

all this is normal

tea and chat and loud clocks

we guess all the tube stops

our bodies grow weary

we need more sleep

we tetris the room to make

room for a bed so one women

who has lost her appetite

can lie next to another

all this is normal

in our bodies are changes

our hearts may not pump as strongly

there's miles davis

playing next to your ear

all of this is normal

our perspective shifts from ourselves

most people are unconscious

we don't know when we are

don't notice time passing

don't feel our bodie

when you are restless

we hold your hands

quiet and gently memories

move round the room

some land on cheeks

we breathe in an unusual way

patterns gradually changing

breath vibrating our voice box

it's not uncomfortable

it's a completely normal

part of dying

hearing is the last sense

why we try to unquiet ourselves

we make a playlist for the last

it's usually very gentle

it just very gently stops

a few minutes later our hearts stop too

KATE

the scientists have been at it again, proving me wrong

they say now that glass is not a liquid but an amorphous solid

the thick parts at the bottom are a fault of design and not a slow drip

I'm sorry I never got to tell you

so you could hold it over me the way I did to you

so proud to be right for the first time

you could crack two nuts in one hand

maybe a boy is a seed and needs to be broken before growing

I wonder if I am an unbroken branch coming out of your cupped hand

I didn't want you to be disappointed so I'll leave nothing out

not even my own madness

you would have wanted me to say dead and not in a better place

in this story there is a boy and his hero

DIFFICULTY SETTING

we write lists and draw star charts

hold ourselves up to them for approval

food comes to the door

like breathing

we drown ourselves and pray for October

October is a traitor   stands at the crossroads

with a crashed car and no apology

London is the world until it sings

all the wrong hymns in your church

an angel grows in your room

at night her halo wakes the house

when she finally rests you know

the difficulty setting of this game is hope

BING

small lit match single bullet in a

turning barrel locked fist it is always

so long between visits you have grown

you will grow I hope you grow well I

am never sure I am much help just a

voice in the distance just an echo when

I reach you I know I should be more

home I know the next chamber will be

blank when I hold you the world stops

ST JOHN'S

Gran smiles when

she sees me

remembers

turns away

sun leaves a trail

through the curtain and

splits the room

in two the nurse

comes in Gran says

don't you think

they're wonderful

kicking me out of

my own home

SPELL FOR MAKING YOURSELF

bring home something alive, turn it sour in the fridge,
turn it sour in the heat, leave it with just enough
sweetness, about as much as death,

hold both your hands to the icy ground, just until they
go blue, the same blue you imagine yourself to be
when drowning, play only one song on repeat
until you hate it, repeat

until tomorrow is a thick fog, become happy but unhealthy,
become thin but sad, run so hard your body gives up,
your body will give up

say you won't do something but do it anyway, bring home
something dead and make it sweet in the fridge make it
sweet in the heat, leave it with just enough sourness
though, about as much as death,

place both your hands to the hot ground until they
burn, the same burn you put into your lungs, hate
one song until you listen to it once, don't
do this again

your body won't last

The first sound
after silence

there are 52 Sundays in a year

Jesus owns all of them

I have never been religious

but when my primary friend

was taken by his dad

I squeezed my hands together

until light couldn't get in

SOLICITUDE

After Kyle Dargan

god grant me the serenity to accept a million magic crystals;
courage to change the money getting divided; and wisdom to
bail out of jail. living one line at a time, enjoying a very strange
reaction, accepting the more I see the more I do as the pathway
to peace, taking something like a phenomenon, this sinful world
as it is, not as a body would come along; trusting what he got will
make all things right if I surrender to go higher baby, so that I may
be reasonably happy in this life and supremely happy to go higher
and higher baby ever in the next. amen.

I'VE GOT FRIENDS I ONLY COMMUNICATE WITH IN REELS

how you been brother like alright still?

for sure life is just happening have you seen the one with the pan lid?

have you heard the one where they dub a man over a goat

yeah yeah I am the goat I am annie are you ok on ice

it's double tap it's hearts on our story hearts on our sleeve

it's 1am it's 6am it's do you ever sleep?

it's late shift morning shift memes no doubt

it's hugs on sight but it's spud it's touch it's I've got your back in a fight

I'm shit at Fifa but I'm that friend I'm drunk I'm drunk

do you need anything from the shop

yeah but I don't think you have the facilities for that big man

infinite ways to watch someone be hit in the head

infinite different items it can happen with

we've probably seen them all

we say lol a lot but it always means lots of love

TU ME MANQUES

in French when something is
missing you say *it is missing from
me*

in hospital you tell me   *everyone's
favourite show is come dine with me
isn't that ironic*

I am in the kitchen scrubbing my
personality out of everything

a boy calling me small somewhere
on the estate where I grew up

I am like pick 'n' mix   none of your
favourite bits in it

being sick with someone can be like
starting a fire   you start small and
build

BONNE NUIT

a heart falls through a heart falls through a heart

our screen time goes up

our step counts

we stand neck high in sting

watch deer run from us

say the moon is full

the woods loud without reason

it starts to tug to pull the sky a cloud we find

a speck of silver in

we fill a room with stout grain glasses up

someone says a pineapple eats you back

I say to lose weight sleep in a bag of pineapple

we laugh   I promise you

when I say were I mean is

when I say was I mean is

SMALL CHOIR
after Selima Hill

on the first day I thought I could

travel by coach I couldn't

I thought if I went back to work

that if I made six phone calls

ate the leftovers

that on the second day

I could

I couldn't

I tried to plan things

sing with a small choir

tell my mum I love her

support arsenal

I couldn't

I thought remembering with friends

would be like the first sound

after silence

it wasn't

SPUDDING A FRIEND WHO'S BEEN AWAY FOR A BIT

the music is turned to 11
fills the estate with childhood
I walk past a van   see a ghost
reach in a fist and say safe bro
love love and all that

heaven is seeing your friend's mum
smile down from three floors up

I'm sure most people don't know
what love is   what forgiveness is

I have only ever seen boys leave
the estate keeps shrinking
it seems like god is pulling
the clingfilm off the people
who pray for him the hardest

so when one comes home
we throw a party till they leave again
drinks spilling off the mantelpiece
the speakers popping from the bass

barbecues filling the air with smoke

we don't care that they won't let us into heaven
we found our own way in

BLANK

blank

wake up

fall asleep

blank

pick it up

put it down

i shouldn't

but why

you're missing the point

blank

back to the start

when was the start

i am losing my days

it's fine

no it's not

blank

roll

then again

fine

then again

try this

it has no effect

blank

sleep is cause and effect

blank

it has no effect

no more relief

maybe this is the end

roll

blank

roll

then again

fine

then again

try this

it has no effect

blank

wake up

fall asleep

blank

pick it up

put it down

i shouldn't

but why

you're missing the point

blank

sleep is cause and effect

blank

back to the start

when was the start

i am losing my days

it's fine

no it's not

blank

it has no effect

no more relief

maybe this is the end

the first time you feel this it will be

infinite

not in a good way

your day will drag like fingernails on chalkboards

you will ask yourself why the sun in a clear sky is ugly

the morning will be an itch you can't scratch

human contact a necessity

the sun will go down

stars will come out

the heavens will be empty

at this point you will in one way or another start again

WHITE CITY

I knew his name and age were both the opposite of senior

I remember how my ears popped and his mother cried

I remember my parents and my body saying go back to bed

in life often there is someone then that someone is dead

we all had our rumours / turned quiet when the police arrived

kicking stones a throw from where his mother grieved

all the parents relegated the toy guns to the bedroom for months

I wonder if they knew what imagery can do to a heart

if they had already practised holding a child for the last time

we couldn't move for handcuffs / the hold on us / silence after

sirens / the absence of boyhood   they only

searched the innocent ones

HOW MANY THINGS WOULD I HAVE TO KNOW

we are sitting on a bench post dinner, my dad says to me I just
don't know it doesn't seem like it will ever end

or we are tucked into a smoking corner of a pub and a friend says
on every side, eventually someone just wants to be racist

or we finish dinner and let the coffee brew a poet says maybe all
the shouting online isn't doing anything but it makes us feel better

my daughter has detached me from my phone broken toy in
hand spotted I'm crying she says can you fix this

LEAVING TO SAY HELLO

all the construction work

that surrounds the Westfield

by my mum's house

or protects Grenfell from memory

creates a hole so big

locals can't dig themselves out

I ask the weed smoke if

the lung it's trapped in

knows its escape is a prison

when they evict the last tenant

how long will they leave them

homeless buried in a fire

that will never stop burning

I DON'T HAVE THE STRENGTH

to watch the boys' names hung like washing

from the balconies of estates   watch yesterday's

dirt fall from them   condolences on a twitter thread

they'll kill us all   say we have no angels

we know wings look like handcuffs

     to those who chewed their spoon to dust

let all the dead boys come back for one last game of five aside

they built our estate temporary   we both tried to be the same

born again out of goodbyes   it doesn't seem right

to pour a glass out in your name   the pubs we left ourselves in

we thought we would be coming back to those churches

where we light a candle at the bar   where the pints smell

like the first time you cried

and a friend held you

STUMBLE

stop now

we are all hurt

we all return to the Earth

there is not enough time to live

just love

just love

like nothing else

matters   say sorry a lot

the sky is coming down dust like

find home

BOTTLE

I wake up every morning

curled into the shape of a beer bottle

and talk myself down off the cap

GOVERNMENT-ALLOTTED WALK

I've been making parts of me so small

they don't need air every other Friday

I hang myself up to dry I am the me I am

in the mirror but not in photos evaporating

in the cascading light   sometimes small

things can be unfolded until they are

unreasonably big of all the things I did

in lockdown I didn't die

LEMONGRASS, APRICOT, BANANA

Colleen Hoover is in the corner explaining

why kids read books with bad sex

and abusive relationships   I don't hear

much but the gist is that our parents

raised us   I am sober   I tell everyone at

the party   once a week I go for an espresso

that costs £4.50 and tastes like blueberry

custard and scoff at the mansions in the

Park   someone asks me where the toilet is

I say there's one on every floor

CANDLES

on the good days I do not pray for it

in the night our bodies find each other

perfectly this year feels like two points

I am moving between I don't know

which is the start I have been ignoring

so many things most of these tasks

are of my making on the zoom

everyone tells me they love me someone

says thank you for chaos I don't know

what I would do if everything was easy

It's not death anymore
just Gary Lineker

When you leave my body

the first time you take a

part of me with you and

every time you enter

you give it back

SOMETHING

and of course you could have died

   i knew that but what use was i

    as the dead weight of my worry

two tiny whirlwinds in the front room

I tried to put it back together

           so that when you finally came down you'd say

you kept it like this for me?

     i'd reply i love you this tidy

instead we cried in the kitchen

    over lukewarm soup

  a week ago we were the people

    in the pictures we look at and sigh

and wasn't it perfect

TODAY SOMEONE WILL ASK ME FOR TOMORROW
AND I WILL SAY YES

I say I want to fuck you

you look at me   like ghosts

haven't risen from us

my lust is a hammer

hitting a gavel   silently

tiny wings beating

there is a haunted house

in my chest most days

the same dream playing on 35mm

I am either a hall of mirrors

or an empty campsite

everyone keeps calling me a fire

leaves rise from the ground

return to trees and I am crying

an ocean is on fire and I am crying

there are church bells

you are too beautiful and I am crying

you are reading me poems

and I am crying   someone has hidden

all the stars under our bed

I am trying not to let you know

CHOPPING WOOD

so basically a man is chopping some wood, a well-built man is chopping some wood, a well-built man in glasses is chopping some wood, I feel every strike in parts of me I didn't know existed, I can't tell if I want to be the axe or the wood or both, I can only tell you there is a well-built man with tattoos, in glasses, chopping wood, I can tell you he says the wood is full of water and is heavy, I am also full of water, I also feel heavier, the man chopping wood is unsure if he will need the wedge, it turns out he doesn't, I can't tell if I really must know what using the wedge is like or not, he says fuck the wedge, he really says fuck the wedge, when the wood is split, each half falling in opposite directions, he turns smiling and throws the axe off camera, straight into my heart.

AND I GUESS I JUST KEEP THINKING ABOUT THE
MICROPLASTICS IN MY PENIS

you know the background music just seems to be pill cases

popping   sharpie ink on foil   I wonder if it would be better

to be walking around with a gun to my head   a gun somewhere

still just unloaded   I can't even listen to music anymore

just podcasts   just people talking and when I close my eyes

and fantasise it's not death anymore just Gary Lineker   I assume

my penis is somewhere in my doomscroll in my daily cake

in my pack of cigarettes at Christmas   know we have never really

touched things   I feel it till my cheeks set fire to themselves

until my whole body is water park   my penis a search bar

serving everything you want with a chaser of regret   I think

my body is punishing me for giving in to less of its whims

the small man in my brain needs a wine needs a line needs

a pill needs just one last dab of a clingfilm wrap   I go

so many nights saying no he stops me fucking

PORTRAIT OF MYSELF AS A STARTED PACK OF
PENGUIN BISCUITS

if a thing has been started

a thing needs to be finished

i am waiting to be consumed

running towards the end

waiting to hit my mark

couldn't stand being the sandal

that narrowly missed Bush

not that i care about Bush

because i wish to be the sandal that hit him

i don't know how clear

i am making myself

what kind of person

wants to be a meteor

that narrowly missed Earth

FIND IT

there is more of you than you know
there is more of you and you do know
there is more of you and you hate it
there's less of tomorrow where you are

I don't know if I can keep
if I can I don't know for how long
somewhere deep there is a voice
that isn't always that deep down

do you remember when we threw
stones at the sky and it popped
ran away as it fell on us
clutching bags full of toothache

one shot two shots all I do is dumb shots
are you okay are you okay
they kicked me out of dirty
they kicked me out of Belushi's

the sky the sea my poems are on fire
this poem is something on fire
when I return myself to my hoodie
and headphones I'll be alright

THIS AIN'T GRAFFITI

Green lung

Pale waves

Waiting for a chance

It started there

Deepfake country

Sunflower thieves

Royal blood

Small talk

Slick fizz

Mosquito

All over again

The wave

Vending machine love

Televised dreams

Hold steady

MIRROR

My whole day day in a jumble

i pull it all out lay it down

the home of my head can be tidy

a memory on a trapeze

a memory jumping through fire

strange when memory is a circus

cup of tea holding it together

stain forming on the inside

teabag falling into the bin

carrying a kangaroo pouch full

my brain breaking into a clown's smile

all the heat lost from my cup

this poem is writing itself

HOLLYWOO

PC as she mourns another heritage she won't give // a difficult conversation in her stomach // a partner who wants too much to love

MPB as he throws money at things that make little sense // an impulsive itch under his skin // all the partners he wants to love too much

DN as she smokes a cigarette on a roof // hiding something from the people she loves // the sadness she tries to love too much

TC as he pretends to be someone he's not // a suit holding in the reality of his world // the one he wants only to love

BH as he sinks all his memories into his liver // everything he regrets trying to drown him // the swimming pool he loved too much

GASP

There's a space inside a space inside
that loves being loved like nothing
I'm a space inside that loves
space that loves a nothing
all this considered
I'm breathing well
I'm breathing
I'm well

I'm

POETRY IS OUR DAD

We say it like that or maybe

like an anchor, like he has fathered us

like there is no God only the writers

we are trying to mirror

how the sky is a mirror of the sea

and drowning is the most poetic way to die

when I was a kid I held the sea next to my heart

like someone close to death

until two boys held me under the same way

when they let go I imagined this was what birth was like

sometimes a poem can feel like this

sometimes I am the sky

and all I want is to be the sea

to have parts of me that have never been seen

I FOLD PRAISE INTO MY POCKET

for when I am better prepared to receive

a thing we all want but can't take

have you ever watched a room leave you

I have been living inside myself

I have been living inside

I have not been letting myself live

sometimes the sky is not a metaphor

is just a thing breaking the night

there is a way out of every stomach

a safe way down   ask the god you pray to

if you don't pray ask the rain ask

the trees ask invention ask me

NORTHERN LIGHTS

147 million kilometres away, a magnetic field
breaches the surface of the sun—a horseshoe
that plasma pulls further from its origin, twists
until it snaps and creates a storm

eighteen hours later, the earth's shield couples
with the storm, not far from a group of excited
tourists, the morning still blurry in their eyes,
and funnels gas into daytime

the storm bends around the earth until
it meets itself and breaks, gas funnelling its way
into nighttime and somewhere, someone
has finally finished searching

Notes

No Man was written in response to the album 'Houses' by Cappo and included in a zine that accompanied the vinyl.

Dying For Beginners is based on a youtube video of the same name by Dr Kathryn Mannix and takes phrases from the video.

Kate was written for my late Grandma and contains some lines from her poem 'Our Story'.

Solicitude is a mash up of 'White Lines' by Melle Mel and 'The Serenity Prayer', which is the prayer you say at the end of AA meetings. It is based on the poem 'The Message' by Kyle Dargan.

Lemongrass, Apricot, Banana takes its name from the tasting notes of the menu at my favourite coffee shop Effy.

Chopping Wood is after a video of Thoren Bradley chopping wood you are welcome.

This Ain't Graffiti is a found poem using the names written on the walls of Nottingham Rough Trade.

ACKNOWLEDGEMENTS

Thanks are due to the editors of *The Alchemy Spoon*, *bath magg*, *Hit Points Anthology* (Broken Sleep Books), *Bi+ Anthology* (fourteen poems), *Ink Sweat and Tears*, *The Poetry Lighthouse*, *Full House Literary Journal*, and *London Grip* who published versions of some of these poems.

Some of these poems appeared in *Blank* and *Solomon's World*.

Immense thanks to my editor Aaron Kent for your insight and support not only on this collection but in life. Thanks for always being there to answer my questions and to send me long voice notes about poetry and Chelsea Football club.

This book might not exist without Yomi Ṣode. I haven't and still don't always know who I am but at a gig Yomi put his arm around me and told me "you are Jake the writer first" I don't think you would be reading this without that moment.

A ridiculous number of poets and friends have been the making of me, whether it's been to give me feedback, a platform to further my career, endorse my work, a shoulder to cry on or a nudge in the right direction. Thank you Matt Cummins, Rikki Livermore, Dean Atta, Deanna Rodger, Antonia Jade King, Peter deGraft-Johnson, Joel Auterson, Tyrone Lewis, Danny Pandolfi, Jenna Omeltschenko, Chris Lanyon, Harry Baker, the staff at Waterstones Nottingham, Caroline Bird, Clare Pollard, Jack Underwood and every single Bad Betty.

To my kids Solomon and Billie, Mum and Dad, Granny Kate and Liz, Grandad Alan, Grandpa Steven and Grandma Susan, Uncle Peter, Auntie Jessica and Rachel, my siblings Izy and Caleb, and the best niece in the world Lucy. To all my Gould / Oakley / Neuer family.

Thank you for keeping me alive Max Frank, Celeste Veazey, and Harry Wills.

Writing this book was only possible because of the love, support, and genius of Amy Acre. There is no one else I could imagine having by my side in business, parenthood and life.

LAY OUT YOUR MORISSETTE